Let's Make Music:
GCSE MUSIC PROJECTS

1 LET'S BEGIN

Trevor Webb
and Nicholas Drewe

Novello

London and Sevenoaks

Cat. No. 11 0209

Trevor Webb acknowledges the assistance and encouragement afforded him by the Kent County Council (Education Committee) in the preparation of this book.

Let's Make Music: GCSE MUSIC PROJECTS

    1: **Let's Begin**
       Cat. No. 11 0209   ISBN 0 85360 129 1

    2: **Let's Go On**
       Cat. No. 11 0210   ISBN 0 85360 130 5

    3: **Let's Listen**
       Cat. No. 11 0211   ISBN 0 85360 131 3

    4: **Let's Listen Again**
       Cat. No. 11 0212   ISBN 0 85360 132 1

    5: **Let's Compose**
       Cat. No. 11 0213   ISBN 0 85360 133 X

Teacher's Pack to include:
Books 1 – 5, Answer Book
       Cat. No. 11 0214   ISBN 0 85360 134 8

available April 1989
    Cassette of 14 extracts (to accompany Books 3 and 4)
       Cat. No. 11 0217

Video: **Let's Make Music**
An exploration of sounds and simple composing techniques, providing basic material for eight class periods.
       Cat. No. 64 0002

Workbook (with Teachers' Notes) to accompany video
       Cat. No. 11 0218

Illustrations: PTA Creative Design, London

ALL COPYRIGHT MUSIC AND TEXT IS SPECIFICALLY EXCLUDED FROM ANY BLANKET PHOTOCOPYING ARRANGEMENTS

Registered office, trade orders, and hire library:
Borough Green, Sevenoaks, Kent TN15 8DT Tel: 0732 883261

Showroom, editorial, retail sales, and mail order:
8 Lower James Street, London W1R 3PL Tel: 01-734 8080

Contents

TREVOR WEBB is Director of Music at Maidstone Grammar School, where he has been particularly concerned with the problems of encouraging teenagers to participate fully in class music. These books have been written as a result of the work done in classes for general music in the 13 – 15 years age-groups, with a firm emphasis on music making. The projects have been shaped towards the demands of the new examinations.

Before going to Maidstone he taught in schools of various kinds, and was for five years Lecturer in Music at Sittingbourne College of Education.

NICHOLAS DREWE was for several years Assistant Music Master at Maidstone Grammar School and has played a vital part in developing the ideas in these books. He is now Director of Music at Eylesden Court School, Bearsted.

To the teacher

LET'S BEGIN is a GCSE workbook, with each chapter studying a different technical topic. Each should be introduced by the teacher with appropriate music to listen to.

The practical work which follows should use as wide a range of sound sources as possible, from electronic instruments and computers to conventional instruments and voices.

Opportunities are given for making scores, and discussions and written commentaries should be encouraged.

1 One, two, one-two-three-four

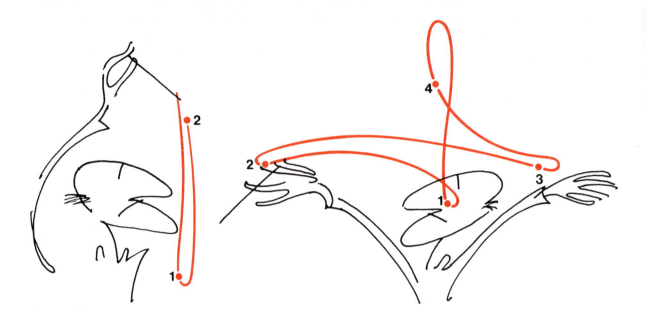

When you listen to music what do you think is most important? Is it the TUNE? The BACKING? Or the BEAT?

The beat is part of the **rhythm** of the music; rhythm is an important part of our daily life:

A heart beat. A ticking clock.

It can be very fast:

The sound of a high-speed train.

It can be very slow:

The changing of the seasons.

Make a list of all the things you can think of in your daily life in which rhythm plays a part.

RHYTHM is more important than anything else in music. That is why the first thing in this book is a chapter about it. Even if you think you know all about it already revise it carefully!

The regular beat of music goes in groups:

The first beat of each group (or **bar**) has a slight accent (>) e.g.

Working in pairs, one person should clap phrases of six to eight bars with 2, 3 or 4 beats to a bar. The other person should say what the beat is.

Long and short notes

Each beat can be split into halves: ♩ = ♫

Say out loud: *Fried bread and ba-con*

Try to get this rhythm: ♩ ♫ ♩ ♩
Clap while you say the words.

Now add: *Saus-a-ges and beans*

♫ ♫ ♩

Each beat can last twice as long: ♩ + ♩ = 𝅝

Try this: *Eggs. Eggs.*

𝅗𝅥 𝅗𝅥

Now put all three rhythms together. Say the words, clap, add instruments; add the rhythms from a drum machine or electronic keyboard as a backing; invent other rhythms and words to go with it. Build a 'Breakfast Picture' in sound. Record your composition and then criticise it carefully.

Things to do:

1 Compose a rhythm piece using today's dinner menu, or the names of your favourite pop groups. Use speaking, clapping, tapping and percussion instruments.
2 Make up a piece to cheer on a games team. Get several different rhythms going at the same time. Use voices, hands, and feet, and make as many different sounds as you can. Remember to vary the amount of sound you make.
3 A rhythm canon: divide into small groups. (The more people you have the harder the game is.) Player 1 begins clapping a simple rhythm. After two bars Player 2 joins in, repeating what Player 1 is doing (but two bars behind). Meanwhile Player 1 goes on to something new which is then copied by the second player. How long can you continue without it going wrong?
4 Set a rhythm going on an electronic keyboard or computer and make up your own rhythms above it. Listen carefully and be sure to keep in time.
5 Compose a piece for these groups of instruments:
   cymbals; woodblocks; drums.
6 Set several keyboards going at once, using different rhythms on each one. Listen to and criticise the results.
   • Can you follow what is happening?
   • Is there a clear beat?
   • Is the result musical?

Pieces to play:

Think of as many ways as possible to play this, using a variety of instruments:

Now a round for three players. Add a keyboard rhythm to keep the beat going. No. 2 starts at the **beginning** when No. 1 reaches figure 2, and so on.

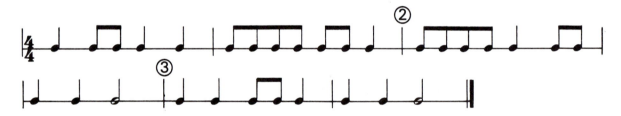

Here, listen for quaver movement passing round the four groups of players. You can repeat each line, or move onto another line each time, until every group has played all four lines.

Quaver Gyrations

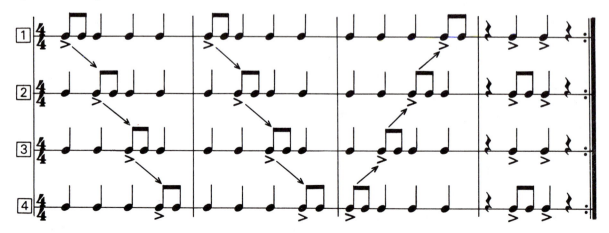

Now Latin American rhythms . . . make them lively!

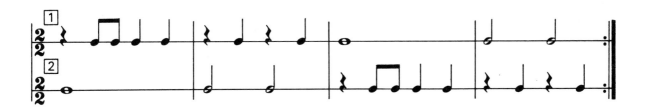

The next piece can be played by one person to a line or as a round. It can be played straight through from beginning to end, or backwards. It can be played with different instruments to each part. When you have mastered it, record it and criticise the results; then try composing your own pieces for rhythm ensemble.

Crescendo for percussion

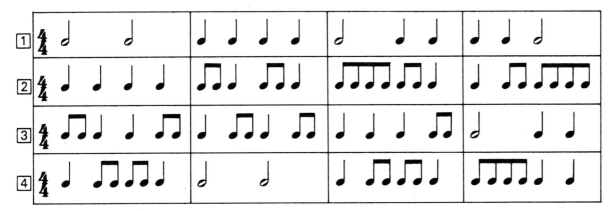

Two 2-part canons

Make these two pieces into canons for three or four players by starting Player 3 in bar 3, and Player 4 in bar 4, in each one.

Canon 1

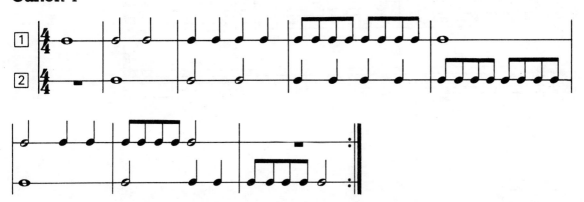

6

Canon 2

Play the following like this:

    1;   1 + 2;   1 + 2 + 3;   1 + 2 + 3 + 4.

Start very quietly and get louder as you go, reaching the loudest point at the end of the second time through. Then get softer, reaching the softest point at the end of the fourth time.

Use a different sound for each part.

Build-up

*Each part
to be played
four times.*

Music to listen to:

Each of these pieces has a strong rhythm in its themes or accompaniment.

Handel: Hornpipe *(Water Music)*
The rhythm of the opening theme plays an important part in the first section of the music:

Bach: *Brandenburg* Concerto no. 2
The last movement opens with this theme:

Chabrier: *España*
This is a Spanish rhapsody and is full of strongly rhythmic dance themes. Here are two of them:

Ravel: *Bolero*
This too is a Spanish dance. The drum rhythm goes on through the whole piece.

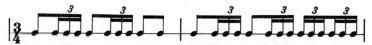

Reproduced by permission of Editions Durand S.A. Paris/
United Music Publishers Ltd.

Bernstein: *America*
This song, from *West Side Story,* has an unusual rhythm:

Reproduced by permission.

Holst: *Mars (The Planets)*
Like Ravel's *Bolero* there is an insistent rhythm:

Mozart: Symphony no. 40
The rhythm of the first theme of the first movement is very important throughout:

2 Fanfares

The Mansell Collection

For centuries fanfares have been used to call people together for important occasions, for ceremonial events, or to give military orders. Berlioz, a nineteenth-century Frenchman, wrote what must be one of the biggest fanfares ever in his *Requiem.* As part of a description of the Day of Judgement he composed a fanfare, and asked for it to be played on 12 trumpets, 12 horns, 4 cornets, 16 trombones, 6 tubas, 16 kettledrums, 2 bass drums, 10 pairs of cymbals and 4 tam-tams. As if that were not enough he added an orchestra and a choir of 250 singers — and the conductor at the first performance hated it so much that he sat down in the middle!

However, you can make a good fanfare out of even one instrument.
Our ancestors used conch shells.
The Romans used trumpets to give commands.
Joshua used trumpets to bring down the walls of Jericho.
Bugles are still used in the army to give orders:

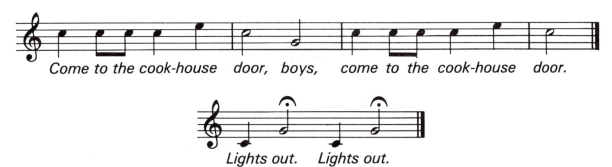

Come to the cook-house door, boys, come to the cook-house door.

Lights out. Lights out.

All instruments used for fanfares work by blowing, to set up a column of air waves inside a tube. But there is a problem; only a small number of notes can be made. If the whole column vibrates in a tube 8 feet long, the note sounded will be:

By tightening the lips and increasing the pressure, the column will vibrate in halves, making this note:

The player can go on splitting the column to make several notes. The lowest is called the **fundamental,** the others **harmonics.** As the harmonics go up, notice how they get closer together:

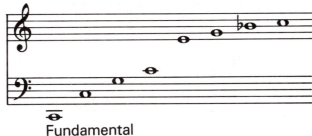

Fundamental

All sounds have harmonics in them at different strengths, and it is the relative strengths which determine whether the sound is that of a violin, a flute, a clarinet, or something quite new such as can be found with a synthesizer.

Things to do:

1 Strike a low piano note hard. Can you hear the harmonics? They can be made easier to hear by holding down the keys of the harmonics without actually playing the notes.
2 Find as many different sounds as you can on a synthesizer. Try to make unusual sounds. Keep a record of the harmonics and their strengths.
3 Using only the notes of the harmonic series based on the note *C*, make up trumpet calls for the following commands. Make the rhythm of the tune fit the rhythm of the words: in that way the command will be easier to remember.

Wake up,   *wake up,*   *get out of bed.*

Breakfast's ready, breakfast's ready.

Put   *your*   *coat*   *on.*

Into   *the Gym*   –   *get*   *changed.*

4 Make up your own commands and calls.
5 Use several instruments, with percussion as well, and compose fanfares for special occasions:
    The opening of a new supermarket
    The beginning of school assembly
What other special occasions can you think of? Invent fanfares for them.

Fanfares to play:

Experiment by using as many different instruments as possible. Add backings (both rhythms and chords) from electronic keyboards; record them; criticise the results.

Fanfare for 2 instruments and timpani

In the next examples choose your own sound for each part, and add percussion parts.

Fanfare 1

12

Fanfare 7

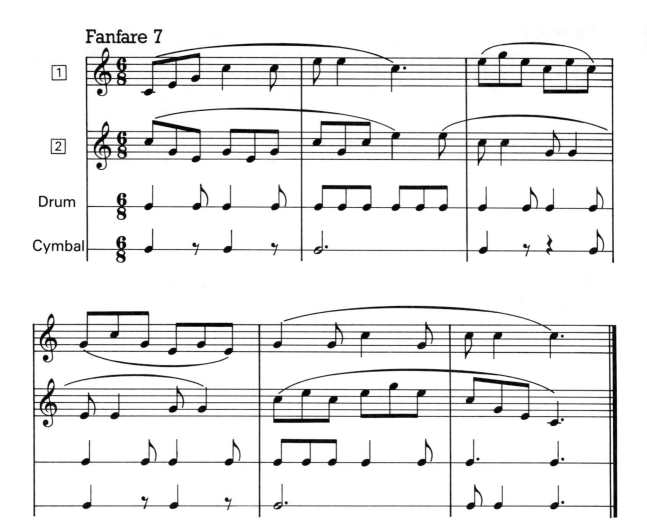

Fanfare 8

3 The three-chord trick

A **chord** is made by sounding two or more notes at the same time.

    SING: Lowest voice: (3) *E D C*

           Middle voice: (2) *G G G*

           Top voice: (1) *C B C*

The Mary Evans
Picture Library

Sing one voice at a time, then two, then all three. Listen to the sounds you make.
Finally, add a fourth voice BELOW, singing *C G C.*
The first chord is a chord of C, the second a chord of G, and the last is the C chord
again.

    Now play these chords on instruments. On an electronic keyboard set the chord
function to 'single finger chord' and press the keys as below:

C then *G*, then *C* again

The guitar symbols are simply 'C' for the C chord and 'G' for the G chord.

    On the stave the two chords look like this:

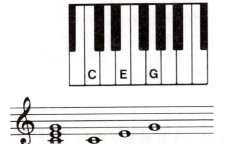

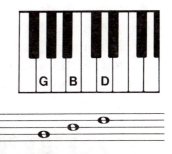

    These two chords belong to the scale of C MAJOR, starting on the first note of
the scale for the C chord and on the fifth note for the G chord. Notice how the
written notes for each are all on the lines of the stave only.

    Adding the F chord enables us to accompany hundreds of tunes. Written down it
looks like this (notice how all its notes are in the spaces only):

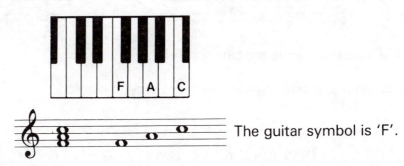

The guitar symbol is 'F'.

Things to do:

1   The three chords C, F and G in C major can be combined to make a 12-bar blues
    sequence:

    1 2 3 4   1 2 3 4

    4/4 C / / / | C / / / | C / / / | C / / / | F / / / | F / / / | C / / / | C / / / | G / / / | F / / / | C / / / | G / / /

    a) Practise the sequence:
        with electronic keyboards: single finger chords.
        on the piano: all three notes in the right hand OR the 'name' note (called the
        root) with the left hand and the other two with the right hand.
        on barred percussion: share the notes between the players.
        You may find it easier to give each player only one chord or one note of a
        chord to begin with. Remember to keep strict time.
    b) Make the sequence more interesting:
        with electronic keyboards: add a rhythm or an arpeggio pattern.
        other instruments: play the root note on the first beat of the bar and play the
        remaining notes on the other beats.
    Repeat the 12-bar sequence as often as you like. To end it satisfactorily use a C
    chord instead of G the last time through in the last bar.
2   Work out the sequence in other keys.

Going further

A chord is made by taking a note as a root; call that note 1. Then find the 3rd and
5th notes above it in the scale in which you are working. Thus the C chord is *C (d) E
(f) G.* In a major scale the chords made on the first, fourth and fifth notes are major
chords. A chord sequence can be made more interesting by using chords made on
the second and sixth notes; these are MINOR chords:

   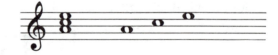

The guitar symbols are Dm and Am.

Play this sequence, using the same ways as before:

4/4 C / / / | C / / / | C / / / | C / / / | Am / / / | Am / / / | Am / / / | Am / / / |

Dm / / / | Dm / / / | Dm / / / | Dm / / / | G / / / | G / / / | G / / / | G / / /

There is one more minor chord, made on the third note on the scale. In C major this chord is Em:

Practise this sequence in the same way as before:

4/4 C / / / | C / / / | C / / / | C / / / | Em / / / | Em / / / | Em / / / | Em / / / |
| F / / / | F / / / | F / / / | F / / / | G / / / | G / / / | G / / / | G / / /

Things to do:

1 Put the last two sequences together and you will have a good Verse-Chorus pattern for a song.
2 Using electronic keyboards explore the effects of different rhythms, accompaniments, and arpeggio patterns. Add improvised rhythms with drums, a drum machine. Link instruments together via MIDI and build up a large-scale composition. Record, or store the result in a keyboard memory. Be critical of what you have done.

The chords you have used can all be made more colourful by adding notes. Try the effect of adding an *A* to the C chord, a *D* to the F chord, and an *F* to the G chord. The guitar symbols are C⁶, F⁶ and G⁷. You will find that G⁷ needs to be followed by C or C⁶.
Revise your earlier sequences using these chords with added notes.
There are four more chords which are very useful in a C major sequence; they add notes which are not in the scale of C, and they are:

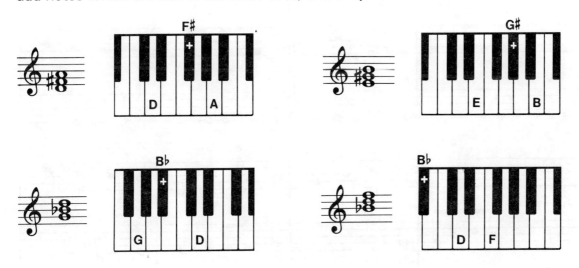

3 Invent sequences, paying special attention to the effect one chord has on another.
4 Using earlier sequences invent melodies to fit them.

A piece to play:

Use a guitar or other instrument, like a synthesizer, which can play chords for the bottom line, and any instruments available for the other lines.

Take Six

Nicholas Drewe

I
C

III
Em

IV
F

V
G

I
C

4 Song maker

With your knowledge of chords you can compose a pop song.

Step one
Think up a story line and condense it into two or three verses. Keep the same number of syllables in each line for all the verses because all the lines will have to fit the same tune.
A separate lyric will be needed for a chorus; this is best kept simple.

Step two
Choose a chord sequence which fits the mood. If it is light and cheerful stick mainly to the MAJOR chords, possibly as simple a sequence as a 12-bar blues. If it is more subdued and serious, work in some MINOR chords. Use only one or two chords for each line, and use a different sequence for the verse and the chorus.

Step three
Find a suitable beat on a drum machine or on the rhythm section of an electronic keyboard and set it at an appropriate speed for the song. Play through the chord sequences. According to the length of each line in your lyric you may need one, two, or more bars of each chord.

Step four
Say your song lyric over the chord sequence. Say the words in different rhythms and with different stresses remembering that you can leave gaps until you find a rhythm that suits. It is now a very small step from saying the words in rhythm to singing them.

Step five

You now have a chord sequence and tune for the verse, and another chord sequence and tune for the chorus. Now decide the overall form (or plan) for the song, that is, the order of the verses and choruses. If you have written three verses then a form like this is suitable:

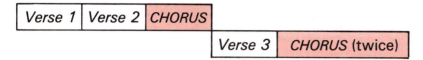

If you have written two verses then you could try this form in which Verse 3 is replaced by an instrumental solo:

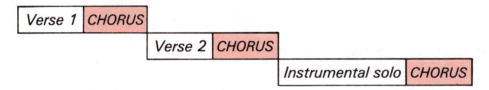

The instrumental solo should keep the chord sequence of the verse, but instead of being sung the solo can be improvised above it.

Step six

From performing the song, you may have noticed that it is difficult to start 'straight in' with the first verse. It is a good idea to compose an instrumental introduction, which is best based on material from the song, possibly the chorus.

Step seven

You may find that the song does not feel right if it stops dead at the end of the last chorus. In recordings, songs are often faded out during repeated choruses; if you are performing your song 'live' this is not really possible. Try these ideas instead:

    i)   Repeat the last line of the chorus a couple of times; during the second, slow down and bring the song to a more natural close.

    ii)   End instrumentally, possibly using material from the introduction.

This closing section is called the **Coda.**

Step eight

REHEARSE — PERFORM — RECORD. Listen to the recording with 'new' ears and criticise it.

- Do the sections follow on from one another naturally?
- Does the tune suit the lyric?
- Is the song the right length?
- Is the overall form satisfactory?

If the answers to all these questions are 'YES', then it might be worth entering the song for a song-writing competition — and who knows . . .?

Things to do:

Follow each stage of this chapter through carefully, and compose a song of your own. Here is a complete set of lyrics for one song to get you started, and a list of further ideas for you to develop.

School Day

CHORUS
It's a school day, not a cool day,
I'd sooner spend the time out with a friend,
It's a school day, not a cool day,
I'll have to sit and dream of next weekend.

VERSE 1
Alarm goes off at seven-thirty,
I do my best to rise at eight,
Throw on some clothes and bolt my breakfast,
I always try not to be late.

VERSE 2
Just miss the bus and have to walk it,
Which seems to be the cue for rain,
Arrive bedraggled and exhausted,
Perhaps I should have caught the train.
                                    CHORUS

VERSE 3
The books I needed I've forgotten,
The teacher gives me extra prep,
And then whilst running to the sports hall,
I twist my ankle on a step.

VERSE 4
School lunch is even worse than usu'l,
The chips are drowning in the grease,
The rain returns throughout the lunch break,
Will school-day problems never cease?
                                    CHORUS

VERSE 5
All afternoon it's hot and sunny,
The classroom seems devoid of air,
The homework set should take all evening,
At times this life seems quite unfair.
                                    CHORUS

Further ideas:

The computer age; Reflections;
The generation gap; World Cup song;
Saying goodbye; A birthday celebration.

5 Modes

Play (or sing) both versions of this melody. The tune, *Orientis partibus*, is a mediaeval French one which was adapted in the nineteenth century to make a hymn tune.

a)

b)

- What changes can you list?
- What do you think is the most important change?

Play the scale used in a) — the earlier version; then do the same for b).

- What is the difference between them?

You have probably come to the conclusion that it is the seventh note which makes the difference, and that this note has made the second version into a major scale. Without this altered seventh note the tune has a less definite ending, and the scale which is used is called a **mode.**

Modes were used for composing until towards the end of the sixteenth century. Since then other scales have come into use, and modes are only part of the modern musical language. They can be found quite easily by beginning on each white note of the piano keyboard in turn, and playing up one octave.

Beginning with *A*, play each mode in turn. What do you notice about the one beginning on *C*?

Write out the modes beginning on *D, E* and *A*.

Things to do:

1 **Composing with modes**
General hints:
i) Give all your melodies a plan (for example, phrase A, phrase B, phrase A again).

ii)   Make your melody revolve round the first note of the mode and end with either the 2nd and 1st notes or the 7th and 8th notes.

iii) Be careful not to mix modes in the same tune.

Set these verses to tunes in either the mode beginning on *D* (the **dorian** mode), or on *E* (the **phrygian** mode), or on *A* (the **aeolian** mode).

a)   *A Boy was born in Bethlehem, in Bethlehem;*
     Rejoice for that, Jerusalem!
     Alleluya, alleluya!

     Phrase plan: A – B – C

b)   *This is the truth sent from above,*
     The truth of God, the God of love,
     Therefore don't turn me from your door,
     But hearken all both rich and poor.

     Phrase plan: A – B – A – C

     Words collected by E.M. Leather.
     Reproduced by permission of Stainer & Bell Ltd.

c)   *The time has come, the Walrus said,*
     To talk of many things:
     Of shoes – and ships – and sealing wax –
     Of cabbages – and kings –
     And why the sea is boiling hot –
     And whether pigs have wings.

     Phrase plan: A – B – A (in pairs of lines).

d)   *The rain it raineth every day,*
     Upon the just and unjust fellow,
     But more upon the just, because
     The unjust hath the just's umbrella.

     From the *Faber Book of Comic Verse*.
     Reproduced by permission.

     Invent your own phrase plan for this one.

2   Modal tunes harmonise well with simple means. Take the first version of *Orientis partibus* and accompany it with a drone bass made by playing *D* and *A* together. These are the first and fifth notes of the mode, and you can use this method to add a drone above or below any modal tune.

    Now make the piece more interesting by adding a simple repeated rhythm, for example:

    Add a countermelody – remember to keep to the notes of the mode of the original tune, so you are limited to *D E F G A B C*.

    Repeat this with the melodies you composed for the verses in a) to d) above.

    Chords for modal pieces are constructed on the same principle as for pieces in ordinary scales. Thus chord I in the Dorian mode would be *DFA*, chord V would be *ACE*, (i.e. 5 notes higher) and so on. Remember there are no sharps or flats!

3　Work out on a keyboard instrument, or a guitar, chords I, IV and V, and end with I. Store your sequence in a keyboard memory, or write it down. Then improvise a modal tune above it. Add percussion and drone effects.

4　Compose a march using a **rondo** pattern: that is, phrase A (8 bars), B (8 bars), A again, C (8 bars), B again, A again. You can make it easier by dividing the work up so that a different person composes each phrase. Begin with a chord sequence, then add a melody.

Modal pieces to play:

1　Personent Hodie

Instruments 2 and 3 have repeated patterns, marked on the score. Choose whatever instruments or electronic sounds you wish for each part. Rhythms can be added from keyboards or drum machines, and a guitar can play the chords. Try putting the completed piece into a computer memory; you could then have a wider range of tone colours for the various parts.

Finally, add another melody to the first part, to sound above it.

Personent Hodie

2 Douce Dame Jolie

This is the melody of a song by the great fourteenth-century French composer Guillaume de Machaut. Compose your own additional parts along the lines of those added to *Personent hodie* above. This tune also is in the Dorian mode.

Douce Dame Jolie

3 The Horse's Branle

This and the next piece come from a dance manual by Thoinot Arbeau, first published in 1588, called *Orchésographie*. He gave this advice:

> "When you dance in company never look down at your feet to see whether you are performing the steps correctly. Keep your head and body erect and appear self-possessed. Spit and blow your nose sparingly."

Notice the design of this piece: A (4 bars), A¹ (4 bars), B (4 bars), B¹ (4 bars), C (4 bars), C¹ (4 bars). After working out your own version as in *Douce Dame Jolie* try composing an original branle; your dance should have two beats in a bar like this one. Try to capture the meaning of the name of the dance: 'branle' comes from a French word meaning 'to sway'.

The Horse's Branle

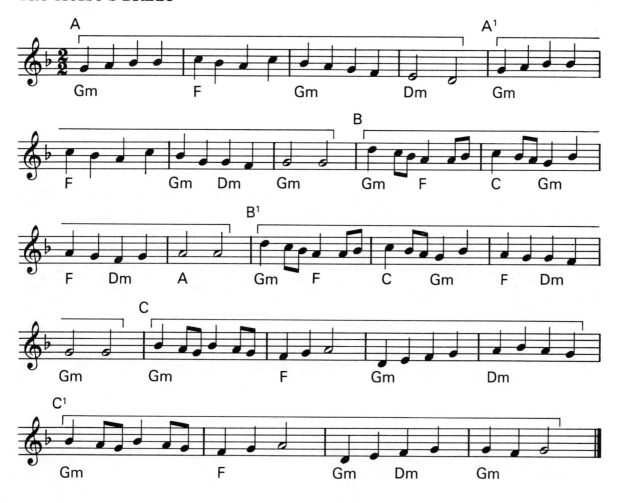

26

4   **Basse Danse 'I will give you joy'**

A basse danse is rather like a branle, but is more serious; the feet were often slid
along the floor rather than lifted up. It is long: 16 bars repeated; another 16 bars;
16 bars repeated, making 80 bars in all. Proceed as for *The Horse's Branle*; you
will have to decide on the pattern of this dance for yourself.

This tune, along with others from *Orchésographie*, was used by the English
composer Peter Warlock in his *Capriol Suite*.

Basse Danse 'I will give you joy'

In your playing and singing you may have noticed that some notes really need to be changed to make the tune or the harmony sound 'right'. Some intervals are awkward:

A tune ending seems to want to change to

Performers at the time that modes were the main musical language regularly changed awkward intervals like these to make them sound better or easier to sing. (This is called **musica ficta**.) Look back at your compositions and decide where changes like these could be made.

In the example *Basse Danse 'I will give you joy'*, the flat signs in brackets are examples of musica ficta. Play the tune without and with the flats.
- Which version do you prefer?
- What is the effect of these alterations and any you have made to your own compositions?

Experiment with changing the seventh note in the mode *G* to *G*, and the fourth note in the mode *F* to *F*.
- What happens to the mode?

6 Call scales

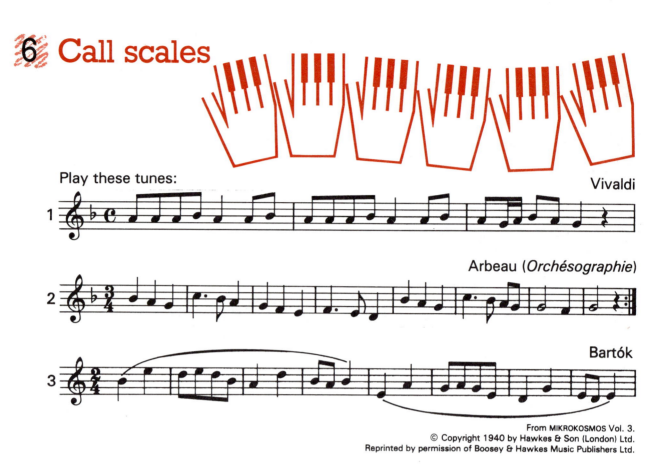

Play these tunes:

Vivaldi

1

Arbeau (*Orchésographie*)

2

Bartók

3

From MIKROKOSMOS Vol. 3.
© Copyright 1940 by Hawkes & Son (London) Ltd.
Reprinted by permission of Boosey & Hawkes Music Publishers Ltd.

Debussy

4

The first tune is in an ordinary major scale, and the second is based on a mode. The other two give us new materials for composing.

The third has a scale made of only five notes: *G A B D E.*

This is a **pentatonic** scale. You can find one easily on the keyboard by playing on the black notes only. But, using the white notes only, you can start with any note as 1; then move up to the next two nearest, to give notes 2 and 3. Skip the nearest note up, and play the next two up, to give notes 4 and 5.

Here are some pentatonic scales to experiment with. Play them until you are familiar with their sounds.

Chinese   *Korean*   *Japanese*

Five-tone Scale

Bartók

Allegro ♩ = 140

From MIKROKOSMOS Vol. 3.
© Copyright 1940 by Hawkes & Son (London) Ltd.
Reprinted by permission of Boosey & Hawkes Music Publishers Ltd.

Things to do:

1 Using this repeated bass improvise a pentatonic melody. Let each player in the group compose a phrase in turn. Agree on a time signature, and on the number of bars in each phrase. Use the notes *C D E G A*.

2 Compose a canon for two players. The second player should try to keep to the same notes as the first. Watch phrase lengths.
3 Compose a pentatonic melody for these words:

> *Old Noah he had an ostrich farm and fowls on the largest scale,*
> *He ate his eggs with a ladle in an egg-cup big as a pail,*
> *And the soup he took was elephant soup and the fish he took was whale,*
> *But they all were small to the cellar he took when he set out to sail,*
> *And Noah he often said to his wife when he sat down to dine,*
> *'I don't care where the water goes if it doesn't get into the wine.'*
>
> G.K. CHESTERTON

Now compose an accompaniment, keeping to the notes of the pentatonic scale you have used for the tune. Add rhythm accompaniment. Work out a phrase plan first.
4 Compose a piece for two instruments or voices called 'Footsteps in the Snow'. Try using two different pentatonic scales, one for each instrument or voice. (You could use a black-note pentatonic scale for one, and a white-note pentatonic scale for the other.) Work out a phrase plan; do not let your music wander or it will not make sense.
5 Look at *Five-tone Scale* by Bartók on page 29. Arrange it in as many different ways as you can think of. For example, the top part could be sung, it could be played on one instrument, or the phrases could be shared out between different instruments. The same treatment can be given to the lower part. Use a synthesizer to create new sounds. Find a subtle rhythm to go with it.

Whole-tone scales

Look back at the melody by Debussy. The scale on which it is based is made up entirely of tones; there are no semitones at all. So it is called a **whole-tone** scale. There are two whole-tone scales:

Which one does Debussy use?
Because there is no 'home note', compositions in this scale can sound very distant and vague.

Things to do:

1 Using the whole-tone scale starting on *C*, compose a tune for the following words. Work to this plan for your first version, then make up your own plans.
   Nothing to do but work!
   Nothing! alas, alack!
   Nowhere to go but out!
   Nowhere to come but back!

2 Use the repeated bass pattern below to improvise a piece in rondo form. (This means that the main theme (A) will keep coming back. A possible plan for the whole piece is A – B – A – C – A.)

3 Compose pieces to represent these ideas:
   A busy town street
   Beside the seaside
   A journey
   Space Invaders
   You will have to decide how to preserve your compositions. The simplest way is to work in short sections and then record on tape. If you decide to write down your work a mixture of ordinary notes on a stave and symbols you invent yourself will be the easiest way.

4 Work in groups of not more than four. Player 1 plays a phrase, Player 2 answers with a phrase of the same length, and so on.

Piece to play:

You need not keep to the instruments shown in *Galactic Journey*.
   The Director is the most important person. He or she must keep the time and tell each group when to begin, without saying anything aloud.
   Each group should practise on its own, with the Director checking to make sure all is right. Then start combining the groups, first with just two and only gradually bringing more in. Keep strict time and do not stop for mistakes. Aim to begin and finish together.
   The notation: Each bar lasts for 5 seconds. Notes written ➤ are played in the

approximate position shown. ➤⌒↘ etc. means start on the note given and then continue in the direction of the arrow.

32

Galactic Journey

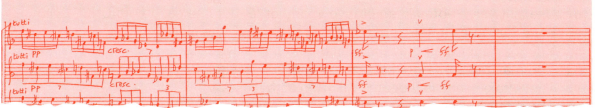

12-note music

This is the violin theme from Berg's *Lyric Suite*:

Extract from Peter Dickinson: *Violin Concerto*

Reproduced by permission of Universal Edition
(Alfred A. Kalmus Ltd.)

Compare it with this tune:

Beethoven: Symphony no. 9, last movement

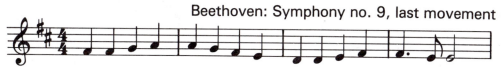

Can you hear these differences:

1 The Berg theme has no definite key; it does not seem to be going to, or need to end on, any particular note. The Beethoven tune begins and ends clearly in a key, in this case D major. In other words, the Berg theme is not written in a conventional scale but the Beethoven tune is.

2 The Beethoven tune keeps only to the notes of the scale of *D*, and repeats them freely. The Berg theme uses all twelve notes to be found in one octave, and other than the three *D* flats in a row it does not repeat any of them.

Now prove this for yourself by playing the Berg theme and marking off the notes as you go on the keyboard:

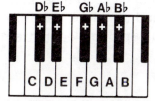

(The black notes are written here as flats rather than as sharps.)

In the early years of this century a group of composers, all born in Vienna, began experimenting with new ways of composing. Their names were Schoenberg, Berg and Webern. Their idea was to write music which had no definite key or scale; instead they used a series of notes made up by using all the twelve notes in an octave, these notes always being used in the same previously decided order. No note was used for the second time (unless it was repeated at once) until all twelve notes had been sounded. The previously decided order (or **series**) used by Berg in the *Lyric Suite* extract is:

1   2   3   4   5   6   7   8   9   10 11 12

34

Before you set about composing with twelve notes, there are some rules which must be kept:

i)   Use all twelve notes in an octave in any order but use each note ONCE ONLY.
ii) Keep the notes in this order all the way through the piece.
iii) You may alter the octave in which a note is played.
iv) You may repeat a note several times in succession.
v)   The whole series is repeated as often as necessary.
vi) The rhythm is up to you.

Things to do:

1   Make your own series. Write each one down in ordinary notes, or put the series into the memory of an electronic keyboard, beginning by listing the twelve notes in order and crossing them off as you go.

2   Use your series to compose melodies. Be sure to give your melodies a plan (for example, A – B – A) so that each one makes sense. Try to express different ideas:

   The haunting
   A fanfare and triumphal march
   A storm
   Computer games
   A summer's day

3   Now orchestrate your melodies. If you are using acoustic instruments assign separate phrases to different instruments. If you are using electronic keyboards assign separate phrases to different sounds. A computer will give you interesting effects if you assign a different sound to each note. Remember to put in expression indications, directions for speed, and so on, to make your notes into real music.

4   Here are some series for you to experiment with. Use each one several times, varying the mood and the style each time as much as possible. Look at Berg's *Lyric Suite* series again, and then look carefully at each of these. You will discover that each is made up of a clear pattern.

Berg: *Lulu*

Schoenberg: *Ode*

Webern: Symphony op. 21

Seiber: *Ulysees*

5 Extend your compositions:
   a) Go through the series backwards.
   b) Turn the series upside-down. To do this, work out the intervals between the notes. If, for example, the interval between notes 1 and 2 is an *ascending* 3rd make it into a *descending* 3rd instead, and so on through the series.
   c) Use b) backwards.
6 As in any other kind of composing, several lines of melody may go on at the same time. Use one of your earlier serial tunes to make canons. Use a different sound for each voice in the canon. Try programming the finished pieces into a computer or electronic keyboard, adding rhythm and percussion effects.
7 Chords may be built in various ways. The easiest is to keep the notes of the series in strict order upwards or downwards:

Webern: Op. 23

Using some of your earlier serial tunes, work out accompanying chords. Space the notes carefully: notes close together will create tension, and notes spaced well apart will be more restful. Use the chords to make the atmosphere you want.
8 Compare your work with music by serial composers, and find out what series has been used in each case. Listen to the whole of Berg's *Lyric Suite* and to Schoenberg's 'Six little pieces for piano' ('Sechs kleine Klavierstücke').

Published by Novello & Company Limited
Printed in Great Britain by The Novelle Press Limited, Borough Green, Sevenoaks, Kent